W9-BGQ-867

animalsanimals

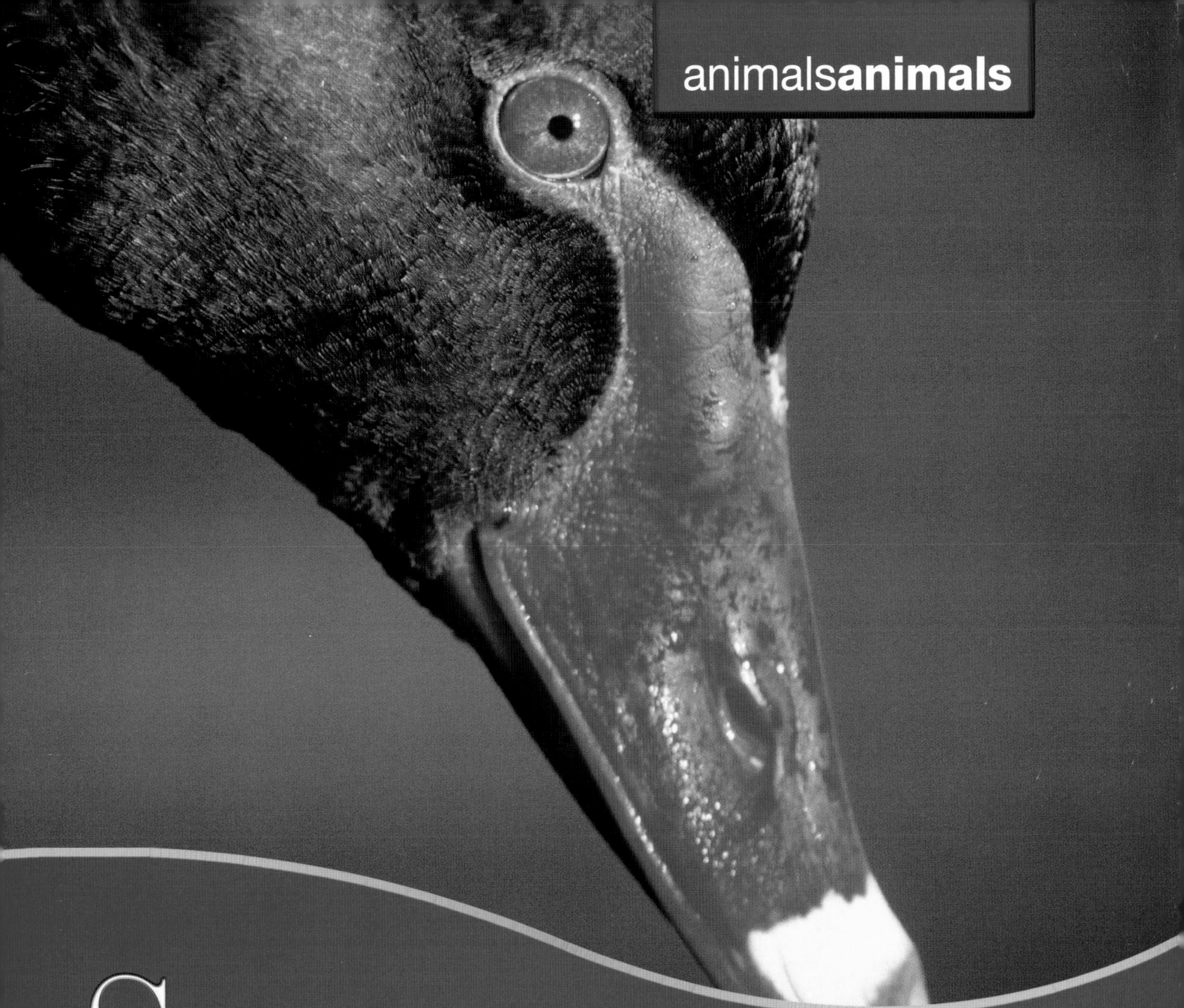

Swans

by **Melissa Stewart**

Marshall Cavendish
Benchmark
New York

Marshall Cavendish Benchmark
99 White Plains Road
Tarrytown, New York 10591-9001
www.marshallcavendish.us

All Web sites were available and accurate when this book was sent to press.

Library of Congress Cataloging-in-Publication Data

Stewart, Melissa.
Swans / by Melissa Stewart.
p. cm. — (Animals, animals)
Summary: "Describes the physical characteristics, habitat, behavior,diet,
life cycle, and conservation status of the swan"—Provided by publisher.
Includes bibliographical references (p. 46) and index.
ISBN-13: 978-0-7614-2530-4
1. Swans—Juvenile literature. I. Title. II. Series.

QL696.A52S75 2007
598.4'18—dc22
2006019716

Photo research by Candlepants Incorporated

Cover photo: Malcolm Schuyl/Peter Arnold Inc.

The photographs in this book are used by permission and through the courtesy of:
Peter Arnold Inc.: Raoul Slater/WWI, 1, 7; Malcolm Schuyl, 4, 33, 42; Cal Vornberger, 6; Manfred Danegger, 22;
John Cancalosi, 23, 31; Steve Kaufman, 24; Lior Rubin, 25; Rupert Buchele/WWI, 26, 34. Minden Pictures:
Yva Momatiuk/John Eastcott, 8; Konrad Wothe, 9, 14; Danny Ellinger, 10; Flip De Nooyer/Foto natura, 20, 41;
Thomas Mangelsen, 36; Jim Brandenburg. Super Stock: age fotostock, 11, 20. Corbis: Darrell Gulin, 12; Kennan Ward, 28;
Raymond Gehman, 38. Getty Images: Pal Hermansen, 18; Peter Macdiarmid, 39; Anselm Spring, 40.

Printed in Malaysia
6 5 4 3 2

Contents

Introducing Swans

"Wow-HOW-oo. Wow-HOW-oo." The wild yodeling calls of tundra swans echo across a Carolina marsh. A moment later, six huge birds cruise into sight.

With their long necks stretched forward and their legs tucked tightly under their bodies, the swans slowly flap their powerful wings. They circle the marsh, looking for a place to land.

Spotting a strip of open water, they spread their wings wide and come in for a landing. At the last possible moment, the birds thrust their feet forward and touch down with a splash.

As swans fly through the sky or glide across the water, their beauty and grace are on full display. But

A tundra swan lets out a loud, long whooping sound.

A tundra swan splashes down after a long, tiring flight.

their large, heavy bodies make takeoffs and landings difficult and clumsy.

Swans are among the largest flying birds alive today. They are closely related to ducks and geese. Their bodies are perfectly designed for swimming and floating on the water's surface. They are excellent fliers as well, but they waddle awkwardly on land because their legs are widely spaced and set far back on their bodies.

By studying *fossils,* scientists have learned that the first swans lived on Earth about 30 million years ago. They made their homes in the lakes, ponds, and *wetlands* of Europe. Over time, swans have spread to mild and cool *climates* all over the world. Today, seven different *species,* or kinds, of swans can be found in North America, South America, Europe, Asia, and Australia.

Seven different swan species live on Earth. Most are pure white, but black swans are found in Australia.

Species Chart

◆ Tundra swans live in North America, Europe, and Asia. True to their name, these birds spend their summers on the arctic *tundra*. Each autumn, they *migrate* to warmer coastal areas. With so much ground to cover, it is a good thing they can fly more than 50 miles (80 kilometers) per hour.

A trumpeter swan.

A mute swan.

◆ At one time, mute swans (above) lived only in Europe and Asia. But people brought them to North America. They often live on lakes and ponds in city parks.

◆ Trumpeter swans (left) live in North America and are the largest swans in the world. They can be as tall as an 8-year-old child and weigh close to 40 pounds (18 kilograms). That's a big bird!

◆ Whooper swans live in the wetlands of Europe and Asia. They are closely related to trumpeter swans, but have yellow markings on their bills.

◆ Black swans (below) live in Australia. They are shaped like mute swans, but have black feathers and a red bill. Black swans prefer to build their nests on mounds in shallow lakes.

A black swan.

A black-necked swan.

◆ Black-necked swans (above) live in the southern part of South America. They have a white body with a black neck and head.

◆ Coscorobas live in the southern part of South America. They are the smallest swan species, and many people think they look more like geese than swans.

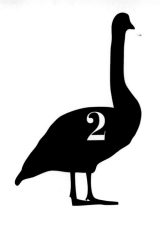

A Swan's Day

2

As the sun slowly creeps above the eastern horizon, the trumpeter swans on MacDonald Pond in southern Montana shake themselves awake. By paddling their webbed feet, the swans glide easily across the water. When they reach the shoreline, the birds begin to feed.

Using their wide, flat bills, the swans tug and tear at arrowhead, bulrush, sedges, and other plants growing near the water's surface. Swans are greedy eaters and can take in up to 20 pounds (9 kilograms) of plants a day.

When a trumpeter swan spots some tasty plants a few inches underwater, it stretches its long neck and

These trumpeter swans are looking for food.

These mute swans are trying to reach tasty plants at the bottom of a pond.

dips down to grab the leaves and stems. Tundra swans prefer to eat the roots of water plants.

When a swan has a beakful of food, it lifts its head out of the water. Then it quickly opens and closes its bill to squeeze out the water. Jagged, tooth-like parts along the edge of the bird's bill trap the food and allow the extra water to drain out.

If few plants are growing on or just below the water's surface, a swan tips its body forward, so that its tail is pointed straight up in

14

the air. Then it can reach more than 3 feet (1 meter) down with its long neck.

In winter, when water plants are in short supply, swans may feed on land, especially if a fresh supply

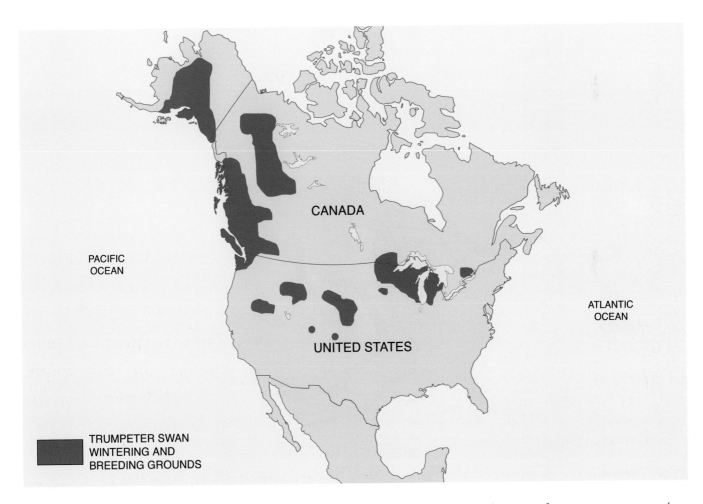

CANADA

PACIFIC
OCEAN

ATLANTIC
OCEAN

UNITED STATES

TRUMPETER SWAN
WINTERING AND
BREEDING GROUNDS

Swans live all over the world. This map shows the winter and summer homes of trumpeter swans in North America.

The Swan:

Swans are awkward on land because their legs are set far back on their bodies . . .

Inside and Out

. . . but they glide through the water with grace.

of grain and seeds is available. Trumpeter swans and tundra swans also eat snails, worms, and other small water creatures when they can find them. Mute swans can eat even bigger *prey*, including frogs and toads.

These mute swans are settling down for the night.

When swans are not eating, they spend much of their time *preening*, or caring for their feathers. Some swans spend up to six hours a day fixing their feathers.

First, a swan pulls each feather through its bill. Like a comb you use on your hair, a bird's bill straightens and moves the feathers so they lie flat. Preening also removes dirt and insects from the feathers.

As a bird preens, it also rubs oil over its feathers. The oil, which comes from a gland near the bird's tail, makes a swan's feathers waterproof. Because water rolls right off a swan's oily feathers, the bird has no trouble staying warm and dry.

Sometimes swans take baths. They hold their wings open and dive underwater. Then they dip and roll along the water's surface. To dry off, they flap their wings and shake their bodies.

By the time the trumpeter swans in MacDonald Pond are clean and well fed, the day is drawing to a close. As the sun sets, the giant birds often settle in the middle of the pond, where land animals cannot disturb them. Each swan coils its long neck across its back and tucks its bill into its wing. Then it closes its eyes and drifts off to sleep.

3 Molting and Migrating

It is nearly noon on northern Alaska's tundra, and the warm, summer sun is high in the sky. Songbirds flit through the air, and shorebirds feed in the wetlands below. But where are the swans?

For most of the spring and summer, visitors can expect to see swans flying above the tundra's gently rolling hills. But for a few weeks in the middle of the summer, the tundra swans huddle together along distant shores and deserted islands. They are *molting*—losing old flight feathers and growing new ones—so they cannot fly.

A swan's wings are covered with layer upon layer of feathers. Both strong and light, feathers help a bird move through the air. Even though swans spend plenty

Tundra swans in flight.

of time preening their feathers, the wear and tear of flight eventually takes its toll. Once a year, the feathers need to be replaced.

Difficult takeoffs and landings can take a toll on a swan's feathers.

At molting time, swans gather in large groups.

Most birds lose their feathers a few at a time, so they can always fly. But swans lose all their flight feathers at once. During the molting period, it is hard for swans to escape from predators. To stay safe, they gather in large groups. With so many eyes watching for danger, predators have a tough time sneaking up on the group.

23

Did You Know . . .
Most migrating trumpeter swans fly about 1,000 miles (1,600 kilometers) twice a year, but some tundra swans travel up to 4,000 miles (6,400 kilometers) from their northern home to their southern one. Most mute swans do not migrate.

By mid-August, tundra swans have returned to the skies—and not a moment too soon. In just a few weeks, the whole group must be ready to migrate to the swans' winter home.

This tundra swan is always on the lookout for danger.

Twice a year, large groups of tundra swans take to the skies for long migrations.

As the days on the arctic tundra grow shorter and colder, the swans feed greedily and gain weight. They will need extra energy to fuel their long flight.

Before their journey, the swans gather in large groups and wait for just the right weather conditions. When a storm moving to the south passes overhead, the swans take to the sky. The storm's strong tailwinds speed the birds' journey to warmer *habitats* with plenty of food.

When spring arrives, the swans return to the arctic tundra. They spend their short, sunny summer raising more young and feeding on the region's rich supply of water plants.

The Cycle of Life

After spending the winter on the outskirts of Yellowstone National Park, a male and female trumpeter swan return to their northern home. The pair has been raising its young at the same Canadian wetland for eight years. Swans often mate for life.

The summer is short and cool, so the trumpeters do not waste any time. They find their nest—high on top of an old beaver lodge—and begin to repair it. The *cob*, or male, collects grass and twigs and passes them to his mate. The female, or *pen*, carefully patches up holes and adds a new layer on top. The pen climbs to the top of the pile and hollows out the center. When she is done, the nest may be 2 feet (0.7 meters) high and up to 6 feet (2 meters) across.

Male and female swans often mate for life.

27

These trumpeter swan eggs are safe in this carefully built nest.

During the next two weeks, she lays up to seven cream-colored eggs. For a little more than a month, the trumpeter pen spends most of her time *incubating* the eggs—sitting on them to keep them warm. Every now and then, she stands up and turns the eggs. This keeps the developing chicks warm and healthy. Tundra swans to the north, and mute swans to the south, perform the same kinds of tasks. Swans all over North America are getting ready for their new families.

When a female swan needs to feed or take a bath, she usually covers the eggs with materials from the nest and then swims away. But the nest is never left unprotected. The female's faithful mate, the cob, stands constant guard. When a hungry predator or another swan gets too close to the nest, the male hisses loudly and swats the intruder with his powerful wings. Most cobs can defend their family from an animal the size of a fox or larger. When the predator has been scared off, the cob and pen celebrate. They face each other, wave their wings, bob their heads, and trumpet loudly.

In early summer, the young swans, or *cygnets*, cheep loudly as they peck their way out of their shells.

When the eggs finally crack open, the little ones pop out, wet and tired. The cygnets quickly find their mother and huddle under her warm body. Soon, the coat of light-gray down feathers covering their bodies dries out and becomes fluffy.

Many newly hatched birds are blind, naked, and weak, but not cygnets. Within a day or two, they

Three young mute swan cygnets get a ride on their parent's back.

Did You Know . . .
Cygnets form a strong bond to the first moving thing they see. Most of the time, it is their mother. But in laboratories, cygnets sometimes *imprint* on, or bond with, people.

A female swan takes good care of her youngsters.

31

begin to swim and feed on their own. Besides water plants, cygnets eat insects and small water animals. These protein-rich foods help the little ones grow quickly.

For the first few weeks of life, the cygnets stay close to their mother. They call to her often during the day and sleep nestled under her wing at night.

By the time the cygnets are about a month old, they have begun to eat the same kinds of plants as their parents. But they will not be ready to fly for another two to three months. During this period, their gray fluffy feathers are replaced by bright white flight feathers.

Cygnets learn to fly in late September or early October. Their first flights are short, but they practice daily until they become strong fliers. Most birds live with their parents for just a few weeks or months and then migrate on their own. Young swans, however, stay with their parents for at least a year.

When the family returns to its northern home the next spring, the parents go to their nest, but the year-old swans do not. They join a large flock of youngsters that spend the summer together.

When the young swans are two or three years old,

This swan family is out for an early morning swim. It will be several more weeks before the cygnets can fly.

Once a male swan finds a mate, he spends almost all of his time with her.

they choose mates during the winter. In the spring, each pair flies to the area where the young pen hatched. The swans choose a territory, but do not build a nest. They spend the summer defending the area, then migrate together in the autumn. They will stay side by side all winter long.

By the following spring, the swans are finally ready to start a family. After the couple mates, the swans build a nest and prepare to be parents for the first time.

The couple may live for another twenty years. During that time, they spend all their time together and repeat the same yearly cycle again and again.

5 Swans and People

When the first Europeans arrived in North America, hundreds of thousands of swans lived in lakes, ponds, and wetlands across the continent. The giant birds with beautiful feathers became a favorite target of hunters.

By the early 1930s, scientists believed that only about seventy trumpeter swans remained in the United States. Tundra swans were doing better because they spent their summers in the far north, where fewer hunters traveled. Meanwhile, settlers brought mute swans from Europe. They began competing with trumpeter swans and tundra swans for food and nesting spots.

Large flocks of trumpeter swans are an unusual sight today, but they were common when the first Europeans arrived in North America.

These trumpeter swans are cruising along the Yellowstone River.

In 1935 the United States government bought a large wetland in Montana and did not allow people to hunt there. Today the area is known as Red Rock Lakes National Wildlife Refuge. As the swan population at Red Rock and nearby Yellowstone National Park grew, scientists moved some birds to the Midwest. Today more than 16,000 wild trumpeter swans live in the United States, and each year the number continues to grow.

But that doesn't mean trumpeter swans are out of danger. In some areas, people still hunt swans even though it is against the law. Swans also die from lead poisoning after accidentally eating lead shot or fishing sinkers. And as more and more wetlands are destroyed to create farmland or construct buildings,

Swans in other parts of the world also face many challenges. These mute swans live close to a European power station that belches smoke all day long.

swans have fewer places to live. Many of the swans that spend their summers in Canada now fly to Red Rock and Yellowstone for the winter. When they join the swans that live in these protected places year round, competition for food can grow fierce. During harsh winters, some birds starve to death. Others catch diseases that spread quickly through the flocks. To solve this problem, scientists now catch Canadian swans as soon as they land at Red Rock and Yellowstone and force them to continue traveling south.

Swans must be studied and protected if their numbers are to increase.

Perhaps one day, scenes like this one will be much more common through-out North America.

Unlike most birds, young swans must learn where to migrate by following their parents. Trumpeter swans that have been moved to the Midwest stay in one spot all year long because in their new habitat, they no longer know when to migrate or where to go. The swans feed in the same lakes and wetlands all

year long, so plants never have a chance to grow back. When the plants die, swans must find other sources of food, or they will die, too.

In an effort to help swans in the Midwest survive, scientists are now trying to train trumpeter swans to migrate. So far, the experiments have had mixed success. But scientists remain hopeful that one day soon, trumpeter swans will once again follow their usual migration routes. Then the mighty birds will have a better chance of surviving far into the future.

Scientists are hopeful that some flocks in the Midwest will again follow the same migration routes they once used.

Glossary

climate—The weather that occurs in a particular place.

cob—A male swan.

cygnet—A young swan.

fossil—The remains or evidence of ancient life.

migrate—To travel a long distance to find food or a place to mate and raise young.

habitat—The place where a plant or animal lives.

molting—Losing old flight feathers and growing new ones.

imprint—In some birds, bonding with the first moving thing the young see after hatching.

incubating—Sitting on eggs to keep them warm.

magnify—To enlarge or make bigger.

pen—A female swan.

predator—An animal that hunts and kills other animals for food.

preen—To care for feathers by cleaning them, straightening them, and rubbing oil on them.

prey—An animal that is hunted for food.

species—A group of similar creatures that can mate and produce healthy young.

trachea—The windpipe or tube that connects the mouth to the lungs.

tundra—A cold, northern region with rolling land-scape and no trees.

wetlands—An area that is covered with water for at least part of the year.

Find Out More

Books

Andersen, Hans Christian. *The Wild Swans.* Cambridge, MA: Barefoot Books, 2005.

Arnold, Caroline. *Birds: Nature's Magnificent Flying Machines.* Watertown, MA: Charlesbridge, 2003.

Horak, Steven A. *Swans and Other Swimming Birds.* Chicago: World Book, 2001.

Miller, Sara Swan. *Waterfowl: From Swans to Screamers.* Danbury, CT: Franklin Watts, 1999.

Osborn, Elinor. *Project UltraSwan.* Boston: Houghton Mifflin, 2002.

Soffer, Ruth. *North American Ducks, Geese, and Swans.* Mineola, NY: Dover, 1996.

White, E. B. *The Trumpet of the Swan.* New York: HarperTrophy, 2000.

Web Sites

The Bird Site: How Does a Wing Work
http://www.lam.mus.ca.us/birds/guide/pg018.html

How Does a Bird Fly?
http://yahooligans.yahoo.com/content/animals/birds/
  birds_howdotheyfly.html

Swans
http://www.feathersite.com/Poultry/Swans/
  BRKSwan.html

Tracking Tundra Swans
http://www.bsc-eoc.org/lpbo/swans/swans.html

The Trumpeter Swan
http://redrocks.fws.gov/rrl3.htm

About the Author

Melissa Stewart has a bachelor's degree in biology from Union College and a master's degree in science and environmental journalism from New York University. She has written more than seventy children's books and numerous articles about animals, ecosystems, earth science, and space science.

Index

Page numbers for illustrations are in **boldface**.